米朝会談後に世界はどう動くか

Spiritual Interview with the Guardian Spirit of Dr. Kissinger

キッシンジャー博士
守護霊インタビュー

英日対訳

RYUHO OKAWA
大川隆法

Preface

We received a spiritual message from the guardian spirit of Dr. Kissinger on September 17, 2016. At that time, contrary to the forecast based on the statistics of all the American mass media, he predicted two months before the Election Day that Trump will become the president. The international headquarters of Happy Science hesitated to publish the content overseas, but the result was exactly what he said. The prophet of today foresaw further than the mass media.

This book talks mainly about how the future will change through the U.S.-North Korea Summit between President Trump and Chairman Kim Jong-un, taken place in Singapore on June 12, 2018. The mass media led by *Newsweek* and others reported that the summit was a landslide victory by Kim Jong-un, but on the contrary, the guardian spirit of Dr. Kissinger said that things are going in a good direction.

まえがき

　キッシンジャー博士には、2016年の9月17日に守護霊霊言を頂いたが、その時彼は、アメリカの全てのマスコミの統計学的な事前予測に反して、投票日の二カ月前にトランプ大統領の誕生を予言した。この内容を英語の本として出版することは、幸福の科学の国際本部も躊躇したが、結果は、その通りとなった。現代の予言者はマスコミの能力を超えたのである。

　本書は、2018年6月12日シンガポールで行われたトランプ大統領と金正恩委員長の米朝会談が未来をどう変えるかを中心に扱ったものだ。キッシンジャー博士の守護霊は、金正恩の圧勝を伝える〈ニューズウィーク〉などに代表されるマスコミとは正反対に、事態が良い方向に前進したことを伝えている。

This shows the same direction that the guardian spirit of Ms. Kim Yo-jong, the real number two of North Korea, and the spirit of former Prime Minister Winston Churchill said in their spiritual interviews which were recorded at around the same time. I am sure I succeeded in shaping the age toward peace. This is the modern book of prophecy that the world is seeking for.

Jun. 22, 2018

Master & CEO of Happy Science Group

President of the Happiness Realization Party

Ryuho Okawa

これは同時期に収録された北朝鮮の実質ナンバー２金キム与ヨ正ジョン氏の守護霊霊言や、ウィンストン・チャーチル元英首相の霊言とも同じ方向を示している。私も平和の方向への時代構築に成功したと考えている。本書こそ世界が求めている現代の予言書だろう。

2018年6月22日

幸福の科学グループ創始者兼総裁

幸福実現党総裁

大川隆法

Contents

Preface 2

1 Asking the Guardian Spirit of Dr. Kissinger,
   the Real Prophet of Today 16

2 Thoughts On the U.S.-North Korea Summit 24

3 Will North Korea Really Denuclearize? 34

4 Will North Korea Open Up to the World? 50

5 Japan Should Revise Their Political Measures
   Against North Korea 58

6 On the U.S.-China Trade War and
   the "One Belt, One Road" Initiative 68

7 The Role of the Happiness Realization Party
   That Was Hawkish to North Korea 78

目　次

まえがき 3

1　現代の本物の予言者・キッシンジャー博士の
　　守護霊に訊く 17

2　米朝首脳会談への評価 25

3　非核化は実現するのか 35

4　北朝鮮という国は変わるのか 51

5　日本は対北朝鮮政策の転換を 59

6　米中貿易戦争と一帯一路構想の見通し 69

7　北朝鮮の脅威を訴えてきた
　　「幸福実現党」の今後の役割 79

| 8 | Japan's National Defense Should be More Than That of France | 90 |

| 9 | On the U.S.-Russian Relations, Middle Eastern Problems and the Loom of a New Superpower | 98 |

| 10 | The Secrets of Dr. Kissinger's Spirit | 114 |

| 11 | After the Spiritual Interview | 124 |

* This spiritual interview was conducted in English. The Japanese text is its translation.

8　日本は「フランス以上の国防力」を持つべき 91

9　米露関係、中東問題、
　　新しい超大国の出現について 99

10　キッシンジャー博士の霊的秘密 115

11　霊言を終えて 125

※本書は、英語で収録された霊言に和訳を付けたものです。

This book is the transcript of a spiritual interview with the guardian spirit of Dr. Henry Kissinger.

This spiritual message was channeled through Ryuho Okawa. However, please note that because of his high level of enlightenment, his way of receiving spiritual messages is fundamentally different from other psychic mediums who undergo trances and are completely taken over by the spirits they are channeling.

Each human soul is generally made up of six soul siblings, one of whom acts as the guardian spirit of the person living on earth. People living on earth are connected to their guardian spirits at the innermost subconscious level. They are a part of people's very souls and therefore are exact reflections of their thoughts and philosophies.

It should be noted that this spiritual message is the opinion of the individual spirit and may contradict the ideas or teachings of Happy Science Group.

本書は、ヘンリー・キッシンジャー博士の守護霊霊言を収録したものである。

　「霊言現象」とは、あの世の霊存在の言葉を語り下ろす現象のことをいう。これは高度な悟りを開いた者に特有のものであり、「霊媒現象」（トランス状態になって意識を失い、霊が一方的にしゃべる現象）とは異なる。

　また、人間の魂は原則として６人のグループからなり、あの世に残っている「魂の兄弟」の１人が守護霊を務めている。つまり、守護霊は、実は自分自身の魂の一部である。

　したがって、「守護霊の霊言」とは、いわば、本人の潜在意識にアクセスしたものであり、その内容は、その人が潜在意識で考えていること（本心）と考えてよい。

　ただ、「霊言」は、あくまでも霊人の意見であり、幸福の科学グループとしての見解と矛盾する内容を含む場合がある点、付記しておきたい。

Spiritual Interview with the Guardian Spirit of Dr. Kissinger

June 18, 2018, at Special Lecture Hall, Happy Science, Tokyo

米朝会談後に世界はどう動くか
キッシンジャー博士
守護霊インタビュー

2018年6月18日　東京都・幸福の科学特別説法堂にて

Henry Alfred Kissinger (1923 ~ Present)

A German-born American and an international political scientist. Received his doctorate from Harvard University and was appointed as a member of the Center for International Affairs. Kissinger served as the assistant to the president for national security affairs and the secretary of state, for both the Nixon and Ford administrations, and promoted reconciliation between the U.S. and China as well as the détente policy between the U.S. and the Soviet Union. He received the Nobel Peace Prize in 1973 for his contributions to ending the Vietnam War.

Interviewers from Happy Science

Kazuhiro Ichikawa
> Senior Managing Director
> Chief Director of International Headquarters

Jiro Ayaori
> Managing Director
> Director General of Magazine Editing Division
> Chief Editor of *The Liberty*
> Lecturer at Happy Science University

Masayuki Isono
> Executive Director
> Chief of Overseas Missionary Work Promotion Office
> Deputy Chief Secretary, First Secretarial Division
> Religious Affairs Headquarters

★ Interviewers are listed in the order that they appear in the transcript.
  The professional titles represent their positions at the time of the interview.

ヘンリー・アルフレッド・キッシンジャー（1923～）

ドイツ生まれのアメリカの国際政治学者。ハーバード大学で博士号を取得し、同大学の外交政策担当教授に就任。ニクソン、フォード両政権で、国家安全保障問題担当大統領補佐官、国務長官を務め、米中和解や米ソのデタント（緊張緩和）政策を推進した。1973年、ベトナム戦争終結への貢献によりノーベル平和賞を受賞。

質問者（幸福の科学）

市川和博（いちかわかずひろ）（専務理事 兼 国際本部長）

綾織次郎（あやおりじろう）（常務理事 兼 総合誌編集局長 兼 「ザ・リバティ」編集長 兼 HSU講師）

磯野将之（いそのまさゆき）（理事 兼 宗務本部海外伝道推進室長 兼 第一秘書局担当局長）

※質問順。役職は収録当時のもの。

1 Asking the Guardian Spirit of Dr. Kissinger, the Real Prophet of Today

Ryuho Okawa Hello, everyone. Today is June 18, 2018, just six days after the recent United States-North Korea Summit in Singapore. I already published urgently, "The Real Number Two of North Korea, Ms. Kim Yo-jong's Real Figure and Power."

And today, I also just published "The Foreign Strategy After the United States-North Korea Conference -A Spiritual Interview with Churchill-"; this is the spiritual teachings of Winston Churchill.

7 Future Predictions: Spiritual Interview with the Guardian Spirit of Henry Kissinger
[Tokyo: HS Press, 2016]

1　現代の本物の予言者・キッシンジャー博士の守護霊に訊く

大川隆法　みなさん、こんにちは。今日は2018年6月18日で、シンガポールでの米朝首脳会談から、まだ6日しかたっていませんが、私はすでに『北朝鮮の実質ナンバー2　金与正の実像　守護霊インタビュー』を緊急発刊し、ちょうど今日は、『米朝会談後の外交戦略　チャーチルの霊言』が出ました。ウィンストン・チャーチルの霊言です。

『北朝鮮の実質ナンバー2　金与正の実像　守護霊インタビュー』(幸福の科学出版刊)

『米朝会談後の外交戦略　チャーチルの霊言』(幸福の科学出版刊)

『ヘンリー・キッシンジャー博士　7つの近未来予言』(幸福の科学出版刊)

1 Asking the Guardian Spirit of Dr. Kissinger, the Real Prophet of Today

Today, I want to summon the guardian spirit of Dr. Henry Kissinger because the Japanese people's belief in, how do I say, the correctness or the effectiveness of the United States-North Korea Summit is almost 50/50. Less than 50 percent, or about 40 percent of the Japanese people *believe* in the effectiveness of this conference. More than 40 percent of the Japanese people *don't believe* in the effectiveness of this conference. Only about 20 percent of the Japanese people believe in the promise of Kim Jong-un. It's not stable now. So, I want to add another spiritual teaching.

We have already been given, *7 Future Predictions by Dr. Henry Kissinger*. It was published two years ago, before my trip to New York that was before the U.S. presidential election. In this book, the guardian spirit of Dr. Kissinger predicted that Donald Trump will be stronger than Hillary Clinton. This was true, and this still is true, so he is the real prophet of today.

I want to know if Henry Kissinger's real opinion

1　現代の本物の予言者・キッシンジャー博士の守護霊に訊く

　今日はさらに、ヘンリー・キッシンジャー博士の守護霊をお呼びしたいと思います。というのは、日本人は、何というか、米朝会談の正当性、有効性について半信半疑だからです。この会談の有効性を信じている人は、日本人の50パーセントまでいかなくて、40パーセントぐらいしかいません。そして、40パーセント以上の人が会談の有効性を信じていないのです。また、金正恩(キムジョンウン)の約束を信じている日本人は20パーセントぐらいしかいません。まだ安定していませんので、霊言をもう一本追加したいと思います。

　私たちは、すでに『ヘンリー・キッシンジャー博士　7つの近未来予言』を頂いています。2年前、アメリカ大統領選挙の前に私がニューヨークへ行く前に出したものです。この本でキッシンジャー博士の守護霊は、「ドナルド・トランプのほうが、ヒラリー・クリントンより強いだろう」と予言しました。そのとおりでしたし、現在もそうですので、彼は、現代の本物の予言者です。
　ということで、ヘンリー・キッシンジャー博士の本心の

1 Asking the Guardian Spirit of Dr. Kissinger, the Real Prophet of Today

is almost the same as that of the guardian spirit of Kim Yo-jong and Winston Churchill or not. It's my guess, but our Prime Minister Abe and our party's* top leader Ryoko Shaku still don't believe in the reality of this promise; they are still waiting for the next stage, what will appear in the near future. They don't believe in these two people's predictions, so I will add another one. This is today's intention.

OK? Then, I will now summon the guardian spirit of Dr. Henry Kissinger. Mr. Ayaori has also interviewed these two people, so this will be the third time. Please give the Japanese people and the foreign people good advice and a direction for our future. Please teach them about that. We will take on this challenge. OK? So then, I will start.

Dr. Henry Kissinger is 95 years old and still living. Before President Donald Trump went on the Asian trip last year, he heard some advice from Henry Kissinger.

---

* "Our party" refers to the Happiness Realization Party (HRP).

1　現代の本物の予言者・キッシンジャー博士の守護霊に訊く

意見が、金与正守護霊やウィンストン・チャーチルと同じかどうか、知りたいと思います。私の推測ですが、安倍首相も、私たちの党（幸福実現党）の釈量子(しゃくりょうこ)党首も、いまだにこの約束が本物であるとは信じてなくて、近い将来に何が起こるか、次の段階を待っています。彼らは、二人の予測を信じていないので、もう一本、追加したいと思います。これが今日の狙(ねら)いです。

　よろしいですか。それでは、ヘンリー・キッシンジャー博士の守護霊を呼んでみます。綾織さんは前の二人にも質問しましたので、これで三人目です。ぜひ、日本と海外の人々に、よきアドバイスと未来の方向性を示してあげてください。それを教えてあげてください。そのことに挑戦したいと思います。よろしいですか。では、始めましょう。

　ヘンリー・キッシンジャー博士は95歳で、ご健在です。去年、トランプ大統領は、アジアを歴訪する前に、ヘンリー・キッシンジャーの助言を受けています。彼は現在でも重要

He is still a very important person, so this is a very important opportunity, I think so. OK? Then, I will call him.

(*Puts hands together in prayer and closes eyes.*)

I want to summon the guardian spirit of
Dr. Henry Kissinger.
The guardian spirit of Dr. Henry Kissinger,
Would you come down here and
Answer our questions?
The guardian spirit of Dr. Henry Kissinger,
Would you come down here, please?

(*About three seconds of silence.*)

人物なので、とても大事な機会であると考えています。よろしいですか。では、呼んでみます。

（合掌し、瞑目をする）

ヘンリー・キッシンジャー博士の守護霊を
お呼びしたいと思います。
ヘンリー・キッシンジャー博士の守護霊よ。
どうかこちらに降りたまいて、
私たちの質問にお答えください。
ヘンリー・キッシンジャー博士の守護霊よ、
どうかこちらにお越しください。
よろしくお願いいたします。

（約3秒間の沈黙）

2 Thoughts On the U.S.-North Korea Summit

Kissinger's Guardian Spirit (*Clears his throat.*)

Kazuhiro Ichikawa Are you the guardian spirit of Dr. Henry Kissinger?

Kissinger's G.S. Hmm. Yeah.

Ichikawa Thank you very much for coming to Japan today.

Kissinger's G.S. I'm old enough, so it's very difficult to fly to Japan. I'm old enough. I do not understand your difficult questions, so please be kind to me, an old man.

Ichikawa Thank you very much. We need your

2　米朝首脳会談への評価

キッシンジャー守護霊　（咳払い)
せきばら

市川和博　ヘンリー・キッシンジャー博士の守護霊様でしょうか。

キッシンジャー守護霊　うん。はい。

市川　本日は日本に起こしくださり、まことにありがとうございます。

キッシンジャー守護霊　私はもういい年なので、日本に飛んでくるのは実に大変なんですよ。いい年なんです。あなたがたの難しい質問はわかりませんので、どうか、年寄りと思って、お手柔らかにお願いします。
てやわ

市川　ありがとうございます。現代の問題に対して、あな

intellectual advice on today's issues.

Kissinger's G.S. Intellectual?

Ichikawa Yes.

Kissinger's G.S. No, just an advice.

Ichikawa Thank you.

Kissinger's G.S. Hahaha.

Ichikawa As you know, our hot issue is North Korea. So, first of all, I'd like to ask you about the summit between North Korea and the U.S.A., between Kim Jong-un and Mr. Donald Trump.

Kissinger's G.S. Oh, OK. It's good. It's nice. I (Dr. Kissinger himself) already advised President Trump.

たの聡明なアドバイスを必要としております。

キッシンジャー守護霊　聡明な？

市川　はい。

キッシンジャー守護霊　いや、ただのアドバイスですよ。

市川　ありがとうございます。

キッシンジャー守護霊　ハハハ。

市川　ご存じのように、北朝鮮がホットな問題になっています。そこで、まず最初にお訊きしたいのは、金正恩とドナルド・トランプ氏の米朝首脳会談についてです。

キッシンジャー守護霊　ああ、わかりました。あれはよかったですね。よかった。私（地上の本人）は前からトランプ

"Firstly, you should use the six-party talks regarding North Korea, and if you fail in this negotiation, the next step should be North Korea and America's direct conference. This is the next step. The result would be difficult, I guess so, but it might be some progressive deed, I think so." I strongly advised him like this. He did it in Singapore, only six days or seven days—I don't know exactly—but about one week ago. This was nice. The fact was nice, I think, firstly. I also want to know the guarantee of the success of this conference and the diplomatic prediction regarding this conference. It might be more than 50 percent success, I guess so.

Ichikawa Thank you very much. You said more than 50 percent.

Kissinger's G.S. Uh huh.

Ichikawa Some people are quite suspicious about this

大統領にアドバイスしていました。「まず、北朝鮮に関する６カ国協議を使いなさい。もし交渉(こうしょう)に失敗したら、次の一手は北朝鮮とアメリカの直接協議です。それが第２ステップです。その結果は難しいものでしょうが、何らかの進展はあるかもしれません」と。私は、彼にそう強くアドバイスしたのです。彼はシンガポールで、それをやったわけです。６日か７日か、正確にはわかりませんが、約一週間前にね。あれは素晴らしかった。素晴らしい事実であると、まずは思っています。この会談の成功の保証と、会談に関する外交的な予測も知りたいものですが、「50パーセント以上の成功」と言えるのではないでしょうか。

市川　ありがとうございます。50パーセント以上と言われました。

キッシンジャー守護霊　うん。

市川　一方で、シンガポールでの米朝合意についてかなり

agreement in Singapore, between North Korea and the U.S.A.

Kissinger's G.S. Of course, of course, of course.

Ichikawa There are no concrete measures for the next process. So…

Kissinger's G.S. The North Korean people and the leaders of North Korea are very difficult people. It's very difficult, even for the United States. Donald Trump, Pompeo, and Bolton, even these people cannot deal with them enough. So, I suggested that some kind of, how do I say, "to-be-generous" attitude is essential, and that it is the first step. "It's more than zero," I said. As the first step, if you can make a platform about the foreign treaty, this platform will be more than zero. It's progressive and hopeful for the future.

懐疑(かいぎ)的な人もいます。

キッシンジャー守護霊　当然、当然、当然です。

市川　次のプロセスへの具体策がありません。ですから……。

キッシンジャー守護霊　北朝鮮の国民と指導者層は、非常に難しい連中ですからね。いくらアメリカであっても、実に難しいのです。ドナルド・トランプやポンペオやボルトン、こうした人たちでも、彼らに十分な対処はできませんので、ある種の、何と言うか、「アバウトな態度」が不可欠であり、それが最初のステップだと提案したのです。「それだけでも"ゼロ以上のもの"だ」と言いました。最初のステップとして、外交上の合意に関するプラットフォーム（土台・基盤）をつくることができれば、そのプラットフォーム自体が"ゼロ以上の成果"です。それ自体が進展であり、未来への希望が持てるものです。

If the American higher post people don't choose this way, they're going to take up some kind of military option. You can easily make a plan on paper, but in reality, it will mean a very fearful result for the future. This is not a TV game; it's real war. Real war means tens or hundreds of thousands of people's deaths, at least. It's a very bad thing to decide too early to fight, so I think this is a good direction.

アメリカの高官たちは、その道を選ばないとすると、何らかの軍事オプションを選択することになるでしょう。紙の上なら計画するのは簡単ですが、現実には、非常に恐るべき結果を招くことになります。テレビゲームではなく、実戦ですからね。実戦では、最低でも何万、何十万という人が死ぬことになるわけです。性急に戦いを決めるのはまずいので、この方向でいいと思います。

3 Will North Korea Really Denuclearize?

Jiro Ayaori We think Kim Jong-un is a devilish person.

Kissinger's G.S. Devilish (*laughs*).

Ayaori I'm sorry.

Kissinger's G.S. OK, OK. That's easy to understand.

Ayaori Do you think he changed his mind? Will he really denuclearize?

Kissinger's G.S. He had no other option. Only the denuclearization policy can guarantee his survival in the political meaning. If he had denied the denuclearization

3　非核化は実現するのか

綾織次郎　金正恩（キムジョンウン）は「悪魔的（あくま）」な人物だと思います。

キッシンジャー守護霊　悪魔的ですか（笑）。

綾織　すみません。

キッシンジャー守護霊　いや、大丈夫です。わかりやすいです。

綾織　彼は考えを変えたと思われますか。本当に非核化を行うと？

キッシンジャー守護霊　ほかに選択肢はなかったのです。彼が政治的に生き残るための保証を得るには、非核化しかありません。非核化を拒（こば）んだなら、彼の国、北朝鮮は、何

policy, his country, North Korea, would be, how do I say, completely perished by Donald Trump. It would be done by nuclear weapons, strong economic pressure, or at least isolation from international relationships. North Korea cannot survive without other countries, so this is his last chance to survive in the future.

Ayaori Do you think Kim Jong-un is going to open up his country from now on?

Kissinger's G.S. It's quite a different problem. It is the first time for them to have their work checked, day by day, week by week, and month by month. It's the first time for them to make their political activity and military activity transparent. It's a dishonorable thing for them. But the international society will watch them. So, in reality, this is the first experience for them. They are very young, but they must welcome it because thanks to the kindness of President Donald

と言うか、ドナルド・トランプによって完全に滅ぼされるでしょう。核兵器か、あるいは大きな経済的圧力か、最低でも国際関係から孤立化させられて、そうなるでしょう。北朝鮮は他国なしでは生きていけないので、これが、彼が今後も生き残るための「最後のチャンス」なのです。

綾織　今後、金正恩は開国に向かっていくとお考えでしょうか。

キッシンジャー守護霊　それは、まったく別の問題ですね。彼らにとって、自分たちのやっていることが毎日、毎週、毎月チェックされるというのは、これが初めてのことです。政治活動と軍事行動を透明化するのも初めてのことです。彼らにしてみれば、不名誉なことなのです。しかし、国際社会は彼らを監視(かんし)するでしょう。ですから、実際、彼らにとっては初めての経験ですし、彼らはまだ若いけれども、この事態を喜んで受け入れなければならないですね。ドナルド・トランプ大統領の温情のおかげで生き延びることが

Trump, they can survive. This is their first trial. I want to recommend them to be honest and to keep being honest. It will save their lives, I mean Kim Jong-un, Kim Yo-jong, and other people, of course.

Masayuki Isono In the recent spiritual interviews with the guardian spirit of Ms. Kim Yo-jong and Sir Winston Churchill, they said that Mr. Kim Jong-un accepted his defeat in the war between the United States and North Korea, and that he surrendered. Do you agree with them?

Kissinger's G.S. Yes, I agree with them because Mr. Kim Jong-un signed the paper between the United States and North Korea. They are aiming for the denuclearization and the peaceful and prosperous future of the Korean Peninsula. So, if they are real politicians or statesmen, it's effective and they will make efforts to realize the assignment.

できるわけですから。初めての試みですが、彼らには「正直であること」「正直さを守ること」を勧めたいと思います。それが、金正恩と金与正、もちろん、ほかの人たちの命を救うでしょう。

磯野将之　先日の金与正氏守護霊とウィンストン・チャーチルの霊言のなかで、二人とも、「金正恩氏は、アメリカと北朝鮮の戦争に関して『負け』を認め、降参した」と語っていますが、賛成されますでしょうか。

キッシンジャー守護霊　はい、賛成です。金正恩氏は、アメリカと北朝鮮の間の文書にサインしましたからね。彼らは、「非核化」と「朝鮮半島の平和と繁栄の未来」を目指しています。彼らが本物の政治家なら、それは効力があるものですし、そうした課題の実現に向けて努力するでしょう。

Isono Thank you. In the joint statement by President Trump and Chairman Kim, Chairman Kim declared that he reaffirmed his firm and unwavering commitment to complete the denuclearization of the Korean Peninsula, but there were no details or concrete plans to denuclearize. That is why many people in Japan and the world are still suspicious. So, in regard to the effectiveness of the joint statement, Dr. Kissinger, what do you think of Mr. Kim's plan to denuclearize North Korea's nuclear weapons?

Kissinger's G.S. If we believe in the capability of Mr. Pompeo and Mr. Bolton, they will make good deals with North Korea and set up a denuclearization plan within three months, and almost all of the nuclear-related facilities, for example, institutions, caves, or hidden bases would be opened. I guess they have more than 300 facilities, so Mr. Pompeo will make the process plan of more than 300 points within two and

磯野　ありがとうございます。トランプ大統領と金正恩委員長の共同声明のなかで、金委員長は、「朝鮮半島の非核化を確実に揺（ゆ）るぎなく完了するために注力することを再確認する」と宣言しましたが、非核化の詳細や具体的な計画には触れませんでした。そのため、日本や世界の人々の多くは、その共同声明の効力について、いまだに懐疑（かいぎ）的です。キッシンジャー博士は、北朝鮮の核兵器の非核化に関する金正恩氏の計画について、どうお考えでしょうか。

キッシンジャー守護霊　ポンペオ氏やボルトン氏の能力を信じるなら、彼らは３カ月以内に北朝鮮にうまく対処し、非核化の計画をつくり上げるでしょう。そして、核関連の施設、例えば、研究所や坑道（こうどう）、秘密基地など、そういったもののほぼ全容が明らかになるでしょう。施設は300以上あると推測しますが、ポンペオ氏は２年半以内に300カ所以上の作業計画を立てるでしょう。この計画が立てば、作業は順調に進むでしょうし、トランプ大統領の最初の任期

half years. If they can set up this plan, the process will proceed smoothly, and at the end of the first presidency of Trump, it will not be reversible. I think so.

Ayaori North Korea has a big military. Will North Korea's military follow Kim's new policy?

Kissinger's G.S. I don't know, but they should obey the order of the top of the country. If not, they will be fired by Kim Jong-un, like how Donald Trump easily fired a lot of officials. Maybe several heads of the military will be fired if they don't want to obey the order of Kim Jong-un.

Isono The guardian spirit of Ms. Kim Yo-jong was worried about the possibility of the assassination of Kim Jong-un and herself by the North Korean military. Do you think this is possible? Do you think that they will be assassinated by their military?

が終わるまでには、不可逆的な状態になるだろうと思います。

綾織 北朝鮮には大きな軍があります。北朝鮮の軍部は金正恩の新たな方針に従うでしょうか。

キッシンジャー守護霊 わかりませんが、国のトップの命令には従うべきでしょう。でなければ、金正恩にクビにされますよ。ドナルド・トランプがたくさんの官僚を簡単に解任(かいにん)したみたいにね。金正恩の命令に従おうとしなければ、軍の幹部が何人かクビになるかもしれません。

磯野 金与正氏の守護霊は、金正恩と自分が北朝鮮軍部に暗殺される可能性を心配していました。ありうると思われますか。軍部によって暗殺されると思われますか。

3 Will North Korea Really Denuclearize?

Kissinger's G.S. Are you expecting an assassination?

Isono No, no, no. I expect a peaceful solution, of course.

Kissinger's G.S. I guess even the North Korean people realized about their foreign policy and foreign affairs through the TV, radio, or newspaper. They know the result of the conference in Singapore, so they understand that if they started the denuclearization of North Korea, it's guaranteed that they will be safe. They will not be attacked by American missiles or nuclear weapons. It's very good for them. They fear about that, so it's also good for them. If they are to choose one of the two, one is the assassination of Kim Jong-un and the other one is the guarantee of the existence of the people or the survival of the people, they will choose the second one. I think so.

3　非核化は実現するのか

キッシンジャー守護霊　暗殺を期待しているわけですか。

磯野　いえいえ、違います。もちろん、平和的解決を望んでいます。

キッシンジャー守護霊　おそらく北朝鮮の国民も、テレビやラジオ、新聞を通して、自国の外交政策や外交問題を理解していると思います。シンガポールの会談の結果も知っているので、「北朝鮮の非核化が始まれば、自分たちの安全が保証される」ということは理解しています。「アメリカのミサイルや核兵器で攻撃されることはない」と。彼らには非常にありがたいことですよ。それを恐れているわけですから、国民にとってもいいことです。「二つのうち一つを選ぶとしたら、一つは『金正恩の暗殺』で、もう一つは『国民の生存、生き残りの保証』である」としたら、後者を選択すると思いますよ。

3 Will North Korea Really Denuclearize?

Ichikawa One more doubtful point about denuclearization is that it takes time.

Kissinger's G.S. Yeah, of course.

Ichikawa It is said that it takes about 15 years. So, even if it's OK while Trump is the president, we don't know what will happen after Donald Trump, or in 15 years.

Kissinger's G.S. Hmm. Yes, there should be some dangerous points, I think so. But even now, if they clash with each other, the U.S. will destroy North Korea. If today, June 18 of 2018, Kim Jong-un denies the promise made at the Singapore conference, the U.S. army can attack North Korea within one month; it means their death. If he denies the denuclearization of North Korea, two years later or three years later, at that time, Donald Trump can destroy North Korea more easily. If there were no Donald Trump and a

市川　もう一つ、疑わしい点は、非核化には時間がかかるということです。

キッシンジャー守護霊　ああ、そのとおりです。

市川　約15年かかるとも言われています。ですから、トランプが大統領である間はいいとしても、トランプ政権後や、15年の間には何が起きるか、わからないのですが。

キッシンジャー守護霊　うーん。そう、いくつか危険な点はあるでしょうね。しかし、今日ただ今でも、両国が衝突すれば、アメリカは北朝鮮を破壊するでしょう。もし今日2018年6月18日に、金正恩がシンガポール会談での約束を反故にしたら、米軍は1カ月以内に北朝鮮を攻撃できますよ。それは「彼らの死」を意味します。2年後、3年後に非核化を否定したとしても、その時点で、ドナルド・トランプはもっと容易に北朝鮮を破壊することができます。その時点でドナルド・トランプがいなくて、アメリカに新たなリーダーが出てきても、次の人物がこの取り決めに

new leader of the United States appears at that time, the next person will obey this commitment and attack or urge North Korea to keep the promise. This is the United States. This is America. This is international politics. This is the world's voice. I think so.

従って、北朝鮮を攻撃するか、約束を守るように促すことになるでしょう。それが合衆国であり、アメリカなのです。それが国際政治であり、世界の声であると思います。

4 Will North Korea Open Up to the World?

Ayaori I would like to ask about China's stance. Is there any possibility that China will not accept Kim's new policy?

Kissinger's G.S. No, no, no. I am the major analyst on China, the first analyst and scholar regarding China and foreign policy. They did a lot regarding this Singapore conference. Xi Jinping only said, "If you meet Donald Trump, just say, 'Stop the United States-South Korea military exercise.' Please say so." Their military exercise, at the same time, means the practice of attacking China. The United States and South Korea have enough military power to attack China. They can fight against China now and conquer their power.

China just started their aircraft carrier strategy. They have only two aircraft carriers, but the American marine

4　北朝鮮という国は変わるのか

綾織　中国のスタンスについてお伺いしたいと思います。中国が金正恩の新政策を受け入れない可能性はあるでしょうか。

キッシンジャー守護霊　いやいやいや。私は中国分析が専門で、中国と外交政策に関する分析家、学者として第一人者ですよ。彼ら（習近平氏と金正恩氏）はシンガポールでの米朝会談に関していろいろしましたが、習近平は「ドナルド・トランプに会ったら、『米韓軍事演習をやめてほしい』と言ってくれ」と言っただけです。この軍事演習には、中国を攻撃する訓練という意味もあるのです。アメリカと韓国で、十分、中国を攻撃する力があり、今すぐにでも中国と戦って勝つことができるのです。

　中国は空母戦略を始めたばかりで、空母はまだ２隻しかありません。しかし、アメリカの海軍力は極めて強大です。

power is a very, very huge one. Even the Japanese Imperial military power was destroyed by them. So, it will be very easy for them. They also have the missile power. If China and the United States attacked each other, China will fail easily because I guess they might only have 400 or around that number of nuclear warheads, but the United States still has thousands of nuclear warheads, so the result is very clear.

Ayaori What do you think of Trump's comments about stopping the joint military exercises? Is this acceptable for you?

Kissinger's G.S. It's a normal way of thinking, I think so, because they, too, are making progressive plans. They need meeting time. So, during that time, they should stop military action. This is a very normal decision.

日本の帝国軍でさえ、米軍に滅ぼされたくらいですから、たやすいものですよ。ミサイルの力だってあるし。中国とアメリカが攻撃し合ったら、中国は手もなく負けるでしょう。中国には核弾頭はおそらく400発ぐらいしかないけれども、アメリカにはまだ数千発もあるので、結果は火を見るよりも明らかです。

綾織　「共同軍事演習をやめる」というトランプのコメントについては、どう思われますか。あなたには受け入れられますか。

キッシンジャー守護霊　当たり前の考え方だと思います。彼らも現在進行形で計画を立てているところですから。話し合う時間も必要なので、その間、軍事行動はストップするべきでしょう。極めて当然の決定です。

4 Will North Korea Open Up to the World?

Ichikawa If North Korea opens up to the world, which way will Kim Jong-un choose as a nation; to be like China, like Russia, or like South Korea? The style of nation. A democratic country, a socialist country, or…

Kissinger's G.S. You mean…

Ichikawa North Korea.

Kissinger's G.S. …what kind of choice?

Ichikawa Choice. For example, Russia opened up to the world and they held general elections, but Putin was elected. Or in China, how it's a socialist country and Xi Jinping is the leader, and there's actually no general election system process. Or in South Korea, there are many parties and Moon Jae-in was elected as the president of the nation. Which kind of style of

市川　北朝鮮が世界に向けて開国した場合、金正恩は国家としてどのような道を選択するでしょうか。中国のような道か、あるいはロシアのような道か、それとも韓国のような道か。国のスタイルとして、民主主義国か社会主義国か、あるいは……。

キッシンジャー守護霊　おっしゃる意味は？

市川　北朝鮮です。

キッシンジャー守護霊　選択の種類ですか。

市川　選択です。ロシアのように、開国して総選挙も実施するけれども、プーチンが選ばれるような体制。あるいは中国では、社会主義で習近平が指導者であり、実質的には総選挙制度はありません。あるいは、韓国には政党がいくつもあり、文在寅が大統領に選ばれました。金正恩はどの国家スタイルを選ぶでしょうか。

nation will Kim Jong-un choose?

Kissinger's G.S. There will be no choice. In these two and half years, Donald Trump should be Donald Trump and Kim Jong-un should be Kim Jong-un. These two people should keep their promise, so no problem. The problem is not of the political regime or election system. The two leaders just decided and they have the responsibility to make them clear and complete. So, I don't know precisely what Donald Trump's thinking in his mind, but I can guess that he will almost finish this deal within his first term of presidency. So, there is no problem about that.

キッシンジャー守護霊　選択の余地はないでしょう。これからの２年半の間、ドナルド・トランプはドナルド・トランプでなければならず、金正恩は金正恩でなければなりません。この二人が約束を守らないといけないわけで、問題はありません。政治体制や選挙制度の問題ではないのです。二人の指導者が決めただけのことであり、それを明らかにし、完全に実行する責任がある。だから、ドナルド・トランプが心のなかで何を考えているか、正確なことは知りませんが、察するに、彼の１期目の大統領在職期間中に、この問題をほぼ終わらせることができると思います。ですから、その点は何も問題ありません。

5 Japan Should Revise Their Political Measures Against North Korea

Ichikawa So next, my concern is the unification of the North and South Koreas.

Kissinger's G.S. Oh, unification is a difficult one, of course.

Ichikawa Can you predict the future of the Korean Peninsula?

Kissinger's G.S. There should be a lot of problems. It's a very difficult one. The first strategy should be the denuclearization of North Korea. Set up a plan and do it. They should do it. As for the process of their denuclearization, South Korea should make negotiations between the North and the South. They will give them some kind of economic aid and another

5　日本は対北朝鮮政策の転換を

市川　そういたしますと、次に、私としては、南北朝鮮の統一に関する懸念があります。

キッシンジャー守護霊　ああ、統一は、やはり難しい問題です。

市川　朝鮮半島の未来については予測がつきますでしょうか。

キッシンジャー守護霊　多くの問題があるでしょうね。非常に難しい問題です。最初にとるべき戦略は「北朝鮮の非核化」でしょう。計画を立て、それを実行することです。それをやらなければいけません。非核化の過程については、韓国が南北間で交渉するべきでしょうね。韓国は、何らかの援助、経済面などで援助を与えるでしょう。

kind of aid.

Kim Jong-un is also thinking about the relation between Japan and North Korea. Mr. Abe, or the one after Mr. Abe, must have some kind of negotiation with Kim Jong-un. At that time, Japan needs to supply some kind of money or materials to North Korea to save the lives of the people of North Korea. They are poor and in a state of poverty. They lack a lot of protein, minerals and other kinds of food, so you, the Japanese people, can do something for them.

Before that, you must decide to make a good relationship between North Korea and Japan. At that time, you must make up your mind regarding the abductees taken from Japan to North Korea. The abductees problem is a very difficult problem. If the North Korean government acknowledges the abductees and have the correct facts, meaning the real number of abductees, if they are alive or not, their names, their families, if they have already passed away or not, then

5　日本は対北朝鮮政策の転換を

　金正恩(キムジョンウン)は、日本と北朝鮮の関係についても考えています。安倍さんか、安倍さんの次の人が、金正恩と何らかの交渉をしないといけません。その際、日本は、北朝鮮の人たちの命を救うために、何らかの金銭や物資の供給が必要になるでしょう。彼らは貧しく、貧困状態にあります。たんぱく質やミネラル、その他の食糧が非常に不足しているので、あなたがた日本人にはできることがあるはずです。

　それに先立って、北朝鮮と日本の間に「良好な関係」を築こうと決意しなければなりません。その際には、北朝鮮による日本人拉致(らち)被害者について決断しないといけません。拉致問題は非常に難しい問題です。北朝鮮政府が拉致被害者を認め、「実際の人数」や「生きているかどうか」「名前」「家族」「すでに亡くなったのか」など、正確な事実を把握(はあく)しているなら、彼らは何とかしないといけません。しかし、おそらく日本人は、彼らの態度や消極的な姿勢に失望するでしょう。ですから、誰かが北朝鮮との間に新たな

the North Korean government should do something regarding that. But I guess the Japanese people will be disappointed at their behavior or negative attitude. Someone should make a new path to North Korea and plan to make a Japanese national policy, for the future.

Ayaori What kind of vision should we have for North Korea?

Kissinger's G.S. "What kind of vision"?

Ayaori The vision of North Korea that we should have.

Kissinger's G.S. "We" meaning just the Japanese or Japan?

Ayaori Japan, the Japanese.

道をつけ、将来に向けた日本の国家としての方針を計画しなければ駄目です。

綾織　北朝鮮に対して私たちが持つべきビジョンはどのようなものでしょうか。

キッシンジャー守護霊　「どのようなビジョン」？

綾織　北朝鮮に対して私たちが持つべきビジョンです。

キッシンジャー守護霊　私たちとは「日本人」ですか。「日本に限って」ですか。

綾織　日本、日本人です。

Kissinger's G.S. (*Sighs.*) It's difficult because Mr. Abe's lifework has been about the abduction from Japan to North Korea. But for them, it's one kind of humiliation because if they admit to that, they would be a kidnapping country or like the Vikings of the United Kingdom around the 10th century. So, it's not so good for them as an independent country.

Mr. Abe will be disappointed at their answer, maybe, but someone should do something about that. I hope your party leader will do something good, give some opinion to your government, or send some message to North Korea. They need another bridge to make a new friendship between the two countries. I guess so.

Isono What kind of message does the Happiness Realization Party need to send to the Japanese government to make a bridge between the two countries?

キッシンジャー守護霊 （ため息）難しいですね。安倍さんのライフワークが北朝鮮による日本人拉致問題ですから。向こうにとっては、一つの屈辱なのです。それを認めたら、北朝鮮は「誘拐犯の国」か、「10世紀頃のイギリスのバイキングみたいな国」ということになってしまいますからね。それは、独立国家として、あまりいいことではありません。

　安倍さんは彼らの回答に失望するでしょうが、誰かがこの問題を何とかしないといけません。あなたがたの政党の党首が何か手を打つとか、政府に提言するとか、北朝鮮に対して何らかのメッセージを発信するとか、そういうことを願いたいですね。両国の間に新たな友情をもたらす「新たな架け橋」が必要だと思います。

磯野　両国の橋渡しをするため、幸福実現党は日本政府にどのようなメッセージを発信していけばよいでしょうか。

Kissinger's G.S. "Be tolerant and future-oriented." It's a key point.

Isono "Be tolerant and future-oriented."

Kissinger's G.S. Uh huh.

キッシンジャー守護霊 「寛容であれ、未来志向であれ」。それが鍵です。

磯野 「寛容であれ、未来志向であれ」と。

キッシンジャー守護霊 そうです。

6 On the U.S.-China Trade War and the "One Belt, One Road" Initiative

Isono OK. Could you give a more specific message? I mean, "be tolerant and future-oriented," we agree, but can you be more specific?

Kissinger's G.S. Japan is one of the largest countries of the world, but your mass media usually looks down on your respectful deed. I mean that you had no resources, but you made a great success from the ruins of the Second World War. It's the pride of the Japanese people, but your mass media thinks little about this success, so the Japanese people also easily forget that they are one of the largest countries of the world. For example, the United States is the number one country in the economic basis and China is the number two, it is said like that. But in the real economic state, I mean the economic strength, Japan

6　米中貿易戦争と一帯一路構想の見通し

磯野　わかりました。もう少し具体的なメッセージを頂けないでしょうか。「寛容であれ、未来志向であれ」というのは賛同いたしますが、より具体的にはいかがでしょうか。

キッシンジャー守護霊　日本は世界最大の大国の一つなのに、日本のマスコミはいつも自国の尊敬すべき行為を見下してばかりいるでしょう。日本は、資源がなくても、第2次世界大戦の廃墟から素晴らしい成功を成し遂げました。それは日本人の誇りであるにもかかわらず、日本のマスコミはその成功に重きを置いていませんね。ですから、日本人も、自分たちが世界の最大国の一つであることを忘れがちです。例えば、経済ベースでは、アメリカが世界一で、中国が2番目だと言われていますが、実際の経済状況つまり経済力では、日本は今なお「世界のトップリーダー」であるのです。

is still the world's top leader.

China should learn a lot from Japan. They are now a large country, but they are still a developing country in many cases. For example, now, China and the United States are struggling regarding the intellectual property problem. China doesn't understand about such kind of problem correctly. They easily use another country's wisdom. For example, they make Seiko or Citizen brand watches, but those are false products. Like that, they make a lot of imitations, but they don't pay the design fee. They are undeveloped in this point.

The EU also suffers a lot from China. There are a lot of imitations of Louis Vuitton and other brands, but the Chinese people don't correctly understand these things. If they want to be a top country or the leading country of the world economy, they should change their attitude in this point. They are thinking or seeking for their profits only and don't think about

6　米中貿易戦争と一帯一路構想の見通し

　中国は、日本から学ぶべきことがたくさんあります。彼らは大国ではあっても、いろいろな面でまだ発展途上国なのです。例えば、今、中国とアメリカは知的財産の問題について争っています。中国は、その種の問題をきちんと理解できず、よその国の知恵を平気で使います。例えば、セイコーやシチズンなどのブランドの時計の偽物をつくっています。そうやって模造品ばかりつくり、デザイン料は払わない。こうした点で遅れているわけです。

　EUも、中国から多くの被害を受けています。ルイ・ヴィトンなどのブランドの模造品がたくさんありますが、中国人には、こうしたことについて正しい理解がありません。世界経済のなかで一流国というか、リーダー国になりたいなら、こうした態度は改めないと駄目です。自分たちの利益を考えて求めるばかりで、ほかの国の利益損失のことは考えないので、日本人の「約束を守る姿勢」や「誠実さ」

the loss of profits of other countries, so they must learn the Japanese promise-keeping or Japanese sincere behavior.

A lot of Chinese people come to Japan and buy a lot of brands and products. It means that the Japanese people are very honest and if Chinese people buy especially higher priced goods at Ginza, they can believe, more than 99 percent, that those are real ones. So, they can believe in Japanese merchandise, but they cannot believe in Chinese merchandise. They are underdeveloped in this point. They easily make imitations regarding machines or other products, so they are under the ceiling. They cannot grow more than they are now. They must learn international promise or custom regarding, for example, trading matters.

Ayaori How do you see the future of the trade war? Is it possible that the Chinese regime will collapse?

に見習わないといけません。

 中国人は大勢日本にやって来て、ブランド品や製品を爆買いしています。それは、「日本人はとても正直だ」ということを意味しています。中国人は、銀座で特別に高い値段のものを買うなら、99パーセント以上、これは本物だと信じることができます。日本の商品は信じることができるのです。しかし、中国の商品は信じることができません。中国人は、この点において遅れているわけです。彼らは、機械や製品の模造品をすぐにつくってしまいます。ですから、彼らには限界があり、今以上に成長することはできません。貿易問題などについて、国際的な約束や慣習を学ばなければいけないのです。

綾織　この貿易戦争の行方についてはどう予測されますか。中国の体制が崩壊する可能性はあるでしょうか。

Kissinger's G.S. The Chinese regime will...?

Ayaori Break down.

Kissinger's G.S. Ah-ha, no, no, no, no. I'm not such kind of a bad prophet. I, of course, have hopes for the Chinese people to make great progress in an honest attitude. They can return enough economic effect to Japan, the United States, and the EU. At that time, in the economic meaning, they can be at the same starting point. So, China needs to change their economic behavior. In addition to that, they, in reality, should change their political system. Some kind of "people first" strategy should be taken in the near future.

Isono Can you foresee the future of the "One Belt, One Road" Initiative of China? What can you foresee?

Kissinger's G.S. It depends. If the Trump Revolution

6　米中貿易戦争と一帯一路構想の見通し

キッシンジャー守護霊　中国の体制が？

綾織　壊れるということです。

キッシンジャー守護霊　ああ、いやいやいやいや。私は、そういう悪い予言者ではないので。私は、もちろん、中国の人々が正直な態度において大いに進歩することを希望しています。彼らは、日本やアメリカ、EUに十分な経済的効果をお返しすることができます。そのとき、経済的な意味において、同じ出発点に立つことができるのです。ですから、中国は、経済における振る舞いを変える必要があります。それに加え、政治体制を実際に変えるべきですね。近い将来、「人民ファースト」戦略のようなものを取り入れるべきでしょう。

磯野　中国の一帯一路構想の先行きについてはどう予測されるでしょうか。何が見えますでしょうか。

キッシンジャー守護霊　状況次第です。アメリカ経済での

regarding the American economy succeeds and Abenomics also does, then it will be difficult to succeed in the "One Belt, One Road" strategy. So, it depends. Japan should start a new economic revolution, I think so.

Isono Thank you.

トランプ革命が成功し、アベノミクスも成功したならば、一帯一路戦略の成功は難しくなるでしょう。ですから、状況次第ですね。日本は、新たな経済革命を始めるべきだと思いますよ。

磯野　ありがとうございます。

7 The Role of the Happiness Realization Party That Was Hawkish to North Korea

Isono I would like to ask you about the future role of the Happiness Realization Party. In 2009, we, Happy Science, established the Happiness Realization Party, and it has sounded the alarm to be careful or be cautious of China and North Korea. "They have very evil intentions. They would attack us, and we are in danger, so be prepared for that. We must build up our defense power." I think that the Happiness Realization Party succeeded to some extent to realize this policy. The Japanese government follows our opinions. But now, it seems that the tide has turned after the Singapore summit meeting, so what kind of role should the Happiness Realization Party play from now on?

Kissinger's G.S. You did well. You made a success.

7　北朝鮮の脅威を訴えてきた
「幸福実現党」の今後の役割

磯野　幸福実現党の今後の役割についてお伺いしたいと思います。私たち幸福の科学は、2009年に幸福実現党を立党しました。幸福実現党は、中国と北朝鮮に注意や警戒をするようにと警告してきました。「彼らは非常に悪しき意図を抱いている。日本を攻撃する恐れがあり、私たちは危機にある。それに備えよ。国防力を固めなければならない」と。そして、幸福実現党は、ある程度、この政策を実現することに成功したと思います。日本政府は私たちの意見に従っています。しかし、シンガポールの首脳会談後、潮目が変わったように見えます。今後、幸福実現党はどういった役割を果たしていくべきでしょうか。

キッシンジャー守護霊　あなたがたは、よくやりましたよ。

7 The Role of the Happiness Realization Party That Was Hawkish to North Korea

The world is indeed following you, so never give up or abandon what you are doing. You are foreseers. The leaders of other countries are just following you. The Japanese government has also been following you these nine years, so be proud of yourselves. You are the reality in Japan and the reality in the Asian area. You can also be the reality all over the world, so be proud of what you did. I think so.

Mr. Ryuho Okawa is the real leader of the world. I (Dr. Kissinger himself) am now 95 years old. I need five more years. I hope so. But I'm old enough, so this might be my last message for you. After this, please depend on Mr. Okawa's opinion. The people of the world, the leaders of the world, please follow him. At that time, you, the Happiness Realization Party and Happy Science, will also take great action, and the people of the world will follow you. You must design the world and please say to the foreign people, "Follow

成功しました。世界はまさに、あなたがたに従っているので、決してあきらめず、投げ出さないことです。あなたがたは、先見力のある人たちです。ほかの国の指導者たちは、ただただ、あなたがたに従っているのです。日本政府もまたこの９年間、あなたがたに従ってきたのです。ですから、誇りに思ってください。あなたがたが"日本の現実"です。アジア地域においてもそうです。"全世界においても、現実になる"ことができます。ですから、これまでやったことを誇りに思ってほしいですね。

　大川隆法氏は、真の「世界のリーダー」です。私（地上の本人）は今95歳で、あと５年生きられたらいいのですが、もう十分に年をとったので、今回があなたがたへの最後のメッセージかもしれません。それ以降は、大川隆法氏の意見を頼りにしてください。世界のみなさん、世界の指導者のみなさん、ぜひ、この方に従ってください。そのとき、あなたがた幸福実現党と幸福の科学も大きな行動をし、世界中の人々があなたがたに続くようになるでしょう。あなたがたが、世界をデザインしなければいけません。そして、諸外国の人々に、「私たちのあとに続いてください。ただ

us, just follow us. We are the next century, itself." You should strongly say so.

Isono Thank you very much.

Kissinger's G.S. Was that Enough? No?

Ichikawa Thank you.

Kissinger's G.S. I'm old, so be kind to me.

Ichikawa Yes. Perhaps the leader of the HRP, Ms. Shaku, will be confident now. Until just two weeks ago, the HRP was quite hawkish to North Korea.

Kissinger's G.S. Hawkish!?

Ichikawa Yes, to destroy North Korea.

ついてきてください。私たちこそ来世紀そのものです」と言ってください。そう強く訴えるべきですよ。

磯野　どうもありがとうございます。

キッシンジャー守護霊　よろしいですか。どうですか。

市川　ありがとうございました。

キッシンジャー守護霊　私はもう年なので、お手柔らかにお願いします。

市川　はい。幸福実現党の釈党首も、たぶん自信を持てることと思います。ほんの２週間前まで、幸福実現党は、北朝鮮に対しては非常にタカ派でした。

キッシンジャー守護霊　タカ派！？

市川　はい。北朝鮮を破壊せよと。

Kissinger's G.S. Oh, I know, I know, I know.

Ichikawa But now, we have to change our mindset to a future-oriented one.

Kissinger's G.S. I know, I know. I've heard this today. "If the guardian spirit of Henry Kissinger denies this meeting, the guardian spirit of Ms. Ryoko Shaku would appear to this table (to send spiritual messages). She wants to say, 'Kill Kim Jong-un. Kill, kill, kill, kill, kill.'" She would say so.

I just came here to stop those words. It's not so good for you and it's not so good for her. So, I'm old enough, but I came here. I'm an old man, but I came here to stop those words.

Don't kill Kim Jong-un. He is the leader of North Korea and he can stop the nuclear weapons program of

キッシンジャー守護霊 ああ、そう、そう、そうでした。

市川 しかし、今や、未来志向の考え方に切り替えないといけません。

キッシンジャー守護霊 そうそう。今日、こんなことを聞きましたよ。「もしヘンリー・キッシンジャーの守護霊が今回の霊言収録を断るようなら、釈量子さんの守護霊がこの場に（霊言をするために）現れるだろう。彼女は、『金正恩(キムジョンウン)を殺せ。殺せ、殺せ、殺せ、殺せ』と言いたがっている」と。彼女はそう言うでしょうね。

　だから、私はその言葉を止めるために、ここに来たのです。それは、あなたがたにとって、そんなによいことではないし、彼女にとっても、そんなによいことではありません。ですから、私はもう十分に年を取っていますが、ここに来たのです。老人ですけれども、その言葉を止めるために、ここに来たわけです。

　金正恩を殺してはいけない。彼は、北朝鮮の指導者であり、北朝鮮の核開発を止めることができるのです。彼は、

North Korea. He is very important now. So, Donald Trump will protect him and keep his word to prevent him from being assassinated.

Ichikawa I'm not sure if it's correct or not, but my understanding is that the HRP is a religious political party, and they should choose and have been choosing the way of "the maximum happiness for the maximum people." Is this correct? In this case, to avoid the war…

Kissinger's G.S. In the near future, it will be correct. But now, you're the opinion party, I think so. You're the party which spreads real opinions or future opinions of the world, and the people of the party are assisting in spreading those opinions. You need a political side as some kind of group, so you're not just a religious group, I think.

You're just thinking about the utopia of the world. You're just thinking about the utopia of China, the

今や非常に重要です。ですから、ドナルド・トランプは、彼を護るでしょう。「彼を暗殺から護る」という約束を守るでしょう。

市川　正しいかどうかはわからないのですが、私の理解では、幸福実現党は宗教政党であり、最大多数の最大幸福への道を選ぶべきであるし、また、選んできました。それで正しいでしょうか。ですから、この場合、戦争を避けるために……。

キッシンジャー守護霊　近い未来、それが正しいということになるでしょう。ただ、あなたがたは、現在は"オピニオン政党"だと思います。あなたがたは、本物の言論や世界の未来についての言論を発信する政党であり、それを広げる支援をしているのが、その党員の人たちですね。あなたがたには、何らかの団体としての政治的側面が必要なので、単なる宗教団体ではないと思いますよ。

　あなたがたは、世界のユートピアについてただただ考えています。中国のユートピアについて、ロシアのユートピ

utopia of Russia, the utopia of Mongolia, Tibet, or Uyghur, and of course the utopia of Iran, Syria, Israel, the EU, or Oceania. So, we just started. You need 100 more years.

7 北朝鮮の脅威を訴えてきた「幸福実現党」の今後の役割

アについて、モンゴルやチベット、ウイグルのユートピアについて、そしてもちろん、イランやシリア、イスラエル、ＥＵ、オセアニアのユートピアについてただただ考えています。ですから、私たちは始まったばかりなのです。あなたがたには、さらに百年が必要ですよ。

8 Japan's National Defense Should be More Than That of France

Isono Could you give us advice on the national defense of Japan? Should we continue or should we stop building up our national defense?

Kissinger's G.S. You need more national defense. For example, more than that of France. I think so. Germany also needs such kind of defense power, I think. If you don't have enough power regarding your defense policy, the North and South Koreas cannot be stable. Russia cannot be stable, China cannot be stable, and the Philippines, Malaysia, and other countries cannot be stable. America needs your defense policy, an effective one.

America is just restructuring their economic policy and building new wealth of the nation, so they need time. I think more than 10 years. We suffered the

8　日本は「フランス以上の国防力」を持つべき

磯野　日本の国防についてアドバイスを頂けないでしょうか。日本は、国防力を高め続けるべきでしょうか、あるいは止めるべきでしょうか。

キッシンジャー守護霊　あなたがたには、もっと国防力が必要ですね。例えば、フランス以上にです。そう思いますよ。また、ドイツも、そのような国防力が必要だと思います。国防政策について十分な力を持っていなければ、南北朝鮮は安定することができません。ロシアも安定できませんし、中国も安定できません。フィリピンやマレーシア、その他の国々も安定できません。アメリカには、あなたがたの国防政策が必要なのです。それも、効果のあるものです。

　アメリカは今、「経済政策の再構築」と「新たな国富の形成」をしていて、時間が必要です。10年以上かかると思います。私たちは二度目の世界的な不況に苦しみました。

second world recession, just 10 years ago; the Great Depression of 1929 and the Great Recession of 2008. Just 10 years later, Donald Trump is still fighting to recover from that kind of recession. After that, America, again, can be a great country. So, America can be America, and America should be America. America can do justice around the world if their economic strategy is effective and if they can survive. From now on, they can be reliable.

Japan, also, should have such kind of responsibility. Great responsibility should be supported by you. So, your party, the Happiness Realization Party, should insist on such kind of great economic strategy for the near future. It's your mission.

Ayaori You said that Japan should be more than France. Do you mean that Japan should or can have nuclear weapons? Do you think so?

ちょうど10年前です。1929年に世界恐慌(きょうこう)があり、2008年にはリーマンショックがありました。それからちょうど10年たちますけれども、ドナルド・トランプは今なお、こうした不況からの回復のために戦っています。それが終われば、アメリカは再び偉大な国になることができるでしょう。つまり、アメリカは、アメリカらしくなれるのです。アメリカは、アメリカであるべきなのです。経済戦略に効果が出て、何とか乗り切ることができれば、アメリカは世界中で正義を行うことができます。今後、アメリカは頼りになりますよ。

　日本もそうした責任を持つべきです。そして、その大いなる責任は、あなたがたによって支えられるべきです。ですから、あなたがたの政党である幸福実現党は、近未来に向けての大きな経済戦略を発信するべきです。それがあなたがたの使命ですよ。

綾織　あなたは、日本はフランス以上であるべきだと言われました。つまり、日本は核兵器を持つべき、あるいは持てるということでしょうか。そう思われますか。

Kissinger's G.S. It's a very difficult problem. But in the near future, Japan will produce nuclear weapons and should join the permanent members of the United Nations Security Council. I hope so.

Isono The Japanese left-wing media criticized Prime Minister Abe's defense policy. For the left-wing media, building up defense power means to make war. But it's not correct, I think. You said to be tolerant and future-oriented. How can we realize or balance building up defense power and making a peaceful relationship between Japan and North Korea?

Kissinger's G.S. Firstly, you should think, "Be independent." Just think about what an independent country is. Be independent. You depend on the United States too much. You depend on the Korean Peninsula status too much. You depend on China's policy too

8　日本は「フランス以上の国防力」を持つべき

キッシンジャー守護霊　それはとても難しい問題です。しかし、近い将来、日本は核兵器を生産するようになるでしょう。そして、国連の常任理事国に加わるべきです。私はそれを望みます。

磯野　日本の左翼マスコミは、安倍首相の防衛政策を批判しています。左翼マスコミは、防衛力の強化は戦争を意味すると思っているのです。しかし、これは正しくないと私は思います。あなたは、寛容さと未来志向と言われましたが、「防衛力の強化」と「日朝間の平和的関係構築」とのバランスを、どのように実現すればよいでしょうか。

キッシンジャー守護霊　まず、あなたがたは、「自立しよう」と考えるべきです。自立した国家とは何であるかを考えてください。自立するのです。あなたがたはアメリカに頼りすぎています。朝鮮半島の情勢に左右されすぎています。中国の政策にも、ＥＵの政策にも左右されすぎています。

much. You depend on the EU policy too much. You should be independent. To be independent, you must listen to a lot of voices from other countries and decide your opinion. Please tell the opinion to the people of the world. That is the real appearance of the world leader, I think. I hope the United States and Japan will lead this century and the next century. China, Russia, and the EU will support the shape of the world. That's good for the world, I think.

あなたがたは自立すべきです。そのためには、外国からの多くの声を聞いて、意見を決定しなければいけません。そして、世界の人々にその意見を語ってください。それが、「世界のリーダー」の本当の姿であると思います。私は、アメリカと日本が今世紀と来世紀を導くことを望みます。中国とロシア、ＥＵが、世界のかたちをサポートするでしょう。それが、世界にとってよいことだと思います。

9 On the U.S.-Russian Relations, Middle Eastern Problems and the Loom of a New Superpower

Ayaori I would like to ask about Russia. How do you foresee the relationship between the U.S. and Russia?

Kissinger's G.S. The U.S. Hmm. The U.S. and Russia.

Ayaori Mr. Trump and Mr. Putin.

Kissinger's G.S. They have the personalities to possibly be friends. Mr. Trump understands Mr. Putin and Mr. Putin also understands Mr. Trump, so they can make a constructive attitude or a treaty between the U.S. and Russia.

But the old-fashioned American people dislike

9 米露関係、中東問題、新しい超大国の出現について

綾織　ロシアについてお訊きします。アメリカとロシアの関係についてはどう予測されるでしょうか。

キッシンジャー守護霊　アメリカ。うーん……。アメリカとロシア。

綾織　トランプ氏とプーチン氏です。

キッシンジャー守護霊　彼らは、友人になる可能性があるだけの人格を持っています。トランプ氏はプーチン氏のことを理解しているし、プーチン氏もまたトランプ氏のことを理解しています。ですから、二人は、アメリカとロシアの間で、建設的な態度や条約をつくることができるでしょう。
　しかし、アメリカの考えの古い人たちはロシアのことが

Russia. That's a problem. These people sometimes criticize Donald Trump. It makes him hesistate to be close friends with Mr. Putin. But a preferable future is where the two guys can be friends, including Mr. Abe or the one after Mr. Abe. It's a better future.

Xi Jinping is taking a 50/50 stance now. He has a great ambition. So, if he survives after Mr. Trump's regime, it still depends, but if a weaker president of the United States appears at that time, the situation will start from scratch. They (the U.S.) must start from zero, so it's difficult.

But never think too much about the darkness of the future. We must start year by year. We must foresee a brighter future, year by year, and think about what we should do this day, this year, and next year. It's an easy step for everyone, I think. Japan cannot see more than one year ahead, so it's very difficult, but only you, I mean the Happiness Realization Party and Happy

嫌いです。それが問題です。こうした人たちがドナルド・トランプをときどき批判するのです。そのため、彼は、プーチン氏と親しい友人になることをためらっています。しかし、好ましい未来は、二人が友人になることです。安倍さん、あるいは安倍さんの次の人も含めて、友人になることです。それがベターです。

習近平(しゅうきんぺい)は今は半々のスタンスです。彼は大きな野望を持っています。ですから、彼がトランプ政権後も生き残ったならば、状況次第ですが、もしそのとき、今より弱いアメリカ大統領が現れたならば、状況は白紙に戻ります。彼ら(アメリカ)はゼロから始めなければいけないので、難しいです。

しかし、未来の闇(やみ)について断じて考えすぎてはいけません。私たちは一年一年スタートしなければならないのです。私たちは毎年、より明るい未来を予見し、「この日、この年、来年、何をやるべきか」について考えなければいけません。これは誰にとっても簡単な一歩だと思います。日本は1年以上先のことは見えないので、非常に難しいでしょうけれども、あなたがた、つまり、幸福実現党と幸福の科学だけは、

Science, can foresee the next 10 years, 30 years, 50 years, or 100 years, so you must be the opinion leader of Japan. If possible, I hope your opinion leadership will prevail on Earth. It depends on the power of the Savior.

Ichikawa Thank you very much. I want to ask about the Middle East issue.

Kissinger's G.S. The Middle East issue.

Ichikawa Mr. Trump moved the U.S. embassy of Israel to Jerusalem, and there is conflict between the Israelis and Palestinians. On the other side, there is an issue of Iran. Mr. Donald Trump denied the Iran nuclear deal. Can you give us any advice, for the future, on the Middle East issue?

Kissinger's G.S. I, myself, is Jewish-German, so it's a

9 米露関係、中東問題、新しい超大国の出現について

次の10年、30年、50年、100年を予測できます。ですから、あなたがたが、日本のオピニオンリーダーにならなければいけないわけです。できれば、あなたがたの言論による指導力が地球に広がってほしいですね。これは救世主の力が頼りなのです。

市川　ありがとうございます。中東問題についてお伺いしたいと思います。

キッシンジャー守護霊　中東問題ね。

市川　トランプ氏は在イスラエル米国大使館をエルサレムに移転しましたが、そこにはイスラエル人とパレスチナ人の対立があります。一方では、イランの問題があります。ドナルド・トランプ氏はイラン核合意から離脱しました。そこで、未来に向けて、中東問題に関するアドバイスを頂けないでしょうか。

キッシンジャー守護霊　私自身、ユダヤ系ドイツ人なので、

sensitive problem even for me. Hmm. The Middle East is very difficult. Now, in 2018, the biggest problem is the nuclear war regarding North Korea, but we are almost 50 percent past it. After that is the nuclear war regarding China. Next to that is, of course, Iran-Israel nuclear war, and another one is Pakistan-India nuclear war. We have these four nuclear war problems. You must clear them, one by one. It's very difficult.

Especially, regarding the Middle East, the Japanese people are apt to think about the oil problem only, but they should know the history regarding the Arabian people and the Jewish people. Their co-existence is a very difficult matter because they already received their mission from different gods. The god of the Middle East and the god of Israel said quite contradictory results. The god of Israel said, "You can conquer the Arabian area because these are yours in the first place." But the Arabian god said, "They are the intruders."

9　米露関係、中東問題、新しい超大国の出現について

　これは私にとっても微妙(びみょう)な問題です。うーん。中東は非常に難しいですね。今の2018年の最大の問題は「北朝鮮に関する核戦争」ですが、この問題はほぼ半分は終わっています。次は「中国に関する核戦争」です。その次は、もちろん、「イランとイスラエルの核戦争」であり、また「パキスタンとインドの核戦争」もあります。私たちは、これら4つの核戦争問題を抱(かか)えているのです。あなたがたは、これらを一つずつ解決していかなければいけません。非常に難しいことです。

　日本人は、特に中東に関しては石油問題ばかり考えがちですが、「アラブ人とユダヤ人の歴史」を知るべきです。彼らの共存はとても難しい問題です。というのも、彼らは、「別々の神」から使命を授かっているからです。中東の神とイスラエルの神は、まったく相反する結論を語りました。イスラエルの神は、「アラブの土地はそもそもおまえたちのものだから、そこを征服(せいふく)してよい」と言いました。ところが、アラブの神は、「彼らこそ侵略者(しんりゃくしゃ)だ」と言っています。ですから、彼らは、この3000年間戦っているわけです。3000年にわたる問題というのは、非常に難しいのです。

So, they have been struggling these 3,000 years. The 3,000-year problem is very difficult. You cannot solve the problem in only one year or two years. Please learn their history.

If Japan can do something for them, reconcile them. Or, give some spiritual message to them to have them accommodate each other. If possible, it's very good. I hope Happy Science accommodates both Israel and the Arabian countries in the name of Elohim*. Both sides, at one time, were governed under the name of Elohim. If you can spread this opinion to them, they can shake hands with each other. I hope so. Religious problems are very difficult. The Japanese people don't look at religious problems, so it's your efforts. You need to make more efforts for the future. But this is a 3,000-year-old problem, so it's not so easy.

---

* The God of the *Old Testament*. Judaism and Christianity consider Elohim to be the same being as Yahweh. However, according to the spiritual investigations by Happy Science, Elohim used to be worshiped in the entire Middle East as the God of love. He is essentially El Cantare, God of the Earth, and a different being from Yahweh, who is an ethnic god. See *The Laws of Faith* [New York: IRH Press, 2018].

9　米露関係、中東問題、新しい超大国の出現について

わずか1、2年では、その問題は解決できませんよ。どうか彼らの歴史を学んでください。

　もし、日本が彼らに対して何かできるとすれば、彼らを和解させてください。あるいは、彼らが和解し合えるように、何らかの霊言を降ろしてください。もし可能なら、とてもいいですね。私は、幸福の科学がイスラエルとアラブ諸国の両者を「エローヒム」の名の下に和解させることを願っています。両者はともに同じ時代、エローヒムの名の下に統治されていました。この見解を彼らに伝えることができれば、彼らは互いに握手することができるでしょう。そう願います。宗教的な問題は、非常に難しいです。日本人は、宗教的な問題を見ていません。ですから、あなたがたの努力です。あなたがたは、未来のために、もっと努力しなければいけません。ただ、これは3000年続く問題なので、そんなに簡単ではないのです。

●『旧約聖書』に出てくる神。ユダヤ教やキリスト教ではヤハウェと同一視されるが、幸福の科学の霊査によると、エローヒムはかつて中東全域で信仰されていた「愛の神」にして、地球神エル・カンターレのことであり、民族神のヤハウェとは別の存在であることがわかっている。『信仰の法』（幸福の科学出版刊）参照。

Ichikawa Thank you very much.

Ayaori Please let us go back to the topic of China.

Kissinger's G.S. Uh huh.

Ayaori Dr. Kissinger in this world proposed that the U.S. and China should form a G2. G2 means the two countries that could divide and govern the world. What do you think of the idea of a G2 as his guardian spirit?

Kissinger's G.S. Hmm. But in the near future, maybe before 2050, there will loom a new superpower. Its name is India. They will compete with China, so the problem is not so easy. America, China, India and Japan, these four countries will make the future story.

If you, the Japanese people, can be friends with

9　米露関係、中東問題、新しい超大国の出現について

市川　ありがとうございます。

綾織　中国の話題に戻りたいと思います。

キッシンジャー守護霊　はい。

綾織　地上のキッシンジャー博士は、「アメリカと中国はG2を形成すべきである」と提案されました。つまり、二つの国で世界を分けるということです。守護霊様としては、G2のアイデアについてどう思われますでしょうか。

キッシンジャー守護霊　うーん。でも、近い将来、おそらく2050年までに、新しい超大国が現れてくるでしょう。その名は「インド」です。彼らは中国と競うので、問題はそんなに簡単ではありません。「アメリカ」「中国」「インド」「日本」、これらの４カ国が未来のストーリーをつくるでしょう。

　もし、あなたがた日本人が、アメリカと友好関係を結ぶ

the United States, with China and with India, you can combine these four countries. But there are other selective strategies, so it's very difficult. It's beyond my opinion, so please ask Mr. Ryuho Okawa about that.

Isono Thank you. In the recent spiritual interview with Sir Winston Churchill, the spirit of Sir Winston Churchill said, "We should have a diplomatic strategy in the age of judgment." What kind of philosophy or policy should we have in living through the age of judgment?

Kissinger's G.S. First one is an old-but-new saying, "Love each other." The first one is, "Love each other." Next one is, "From the eyes of God, judge justice and evil." If you can tell justice from evil, please make effort to choose justice and forget about evil or throw

9 米露関係、中東問題、新しい超大国の出現について

ことができ、中国と友好関係を結ぶことができ、インドと友好関係を結ぶことができれば、あなたがたは、これらの4カ国を結びつけることができます。しかし、ほかにも選択可能な戦略があるでしょうから、非常に難しいでしょう。これについては、私の任を超えているので、大川隆法氏に訊いてください。

磯野　ありがとうございます。最近、ウィンストン・チャーチルは、その霊言のなかで、「私たちは、判断の時代の外交戦略を持つべきだ」とおっしゃっていました。この判断の時代を生き抜くためには、どのような思想や指針を持つべきでしょうか。

キッシンジャー守護霊　1番目のポイントは、古くて新しい格言で、「互いに愛し合え」ということです。まずは「互いに愛し合え」で、次は「神の目から見て、正義と悪を判断しなさい」ということです。そして、正義と悪を区別することができたら、どうか正義を選び、悪については忘れ、

away evil. This is the second point. The third point is, "There are a lot of species, colors, and nationalities, but all of you are earthlings, I mean the people of Earth, so in the name of Earth, you must unite, cooperate and co-survive." It is your mission. I think so. "Love each other," "Tell bad from good," and "Build your belief from the standpoint of earthlings." These three points are very essential.

One problem is the differences in religion, but it's up to you, Happy Science. Please overcome the difficulties and the walls of discrimination regarding religion and species. You have universal love and universal brotherhood. You can believe in them. These will make you strong and make your planet greater and greater.

I cannot say any more because I am just a 95-year-old American. It's not good for me to say more than this. If I say that, I would be a savior, so I cannot say any more. It's my limit (*laughs*).

悪を捨て去るように努力してください。これが２番目のポイントです。３番目のポイントは、「人種や肌の色、国籍などがさまざまにあるけれども、あなたがたはみな地球人であり、地球の名の下に団結し、協力し、ともに生き延びていかなければならない」ということです。これは、あなたがたの使命だと思います。「互いに愛し合え」「善悪を区別せよ」「地球人の立場から信仰を立てよ」ということです。この３つのポイントが非常に重要です。

　一つ問題があるとするなら宗教の違いですが、それは、あなたがた幸福の科学にかかっています。どうか困難を乗り越え、「宗教や人種の差別の壁」を超えていってください。あなたがたには、普遍的な愛、普遍的な同胞愛があります。あなたがたはそれを信じることができるのです。それが、あなたがたを強くし、この惑星をより偉大にするでしょう。

　これ以上は言えません。私は95歳の年老いたアメリカ人なのでね。これ以上話すのは、私にとってよくないのです。もしそれを言えば、私は救世主ということになるので、これ以上は言えないのです。私の限界です（笑）。

10 The Secrets of Dr. Kissinger's Spirit

Ichikawa Thank you very much. The time is almost up. Mr. Ayaori, do you have any last question?

Kissinger's G.S. Is it OK? One more?

Ayaori I think your comments are based on very deep insight. Could you share the secrets of your spirit?

Kissinger's G.S. The secret of my spirit?

Ayaori Yes.

Kissinger's G.S. Ah, hmm. Of course, I'm good at studying foreign policy as a scholar and as a statesman.

10　キッシンジャー博士の霊的秘密

市川　ありがとうございます。そろそろお時間が迫ってまいりました。綾織さん、最後に質問したいことはありますか。

キッシンジャー守護霊　これでよろしいですか。もう一つ？

綾織　あなたのご意見は、とても深い洞察(どうさつ)に基づいていると思います。あなたの霊の秘密を明かしていただけないでしょうか。

キッシンジャー守護霊　霊の秘密？

綾織　はい。

キッシンジャー守護霊　ああ、うーん。もちろん、私は、学者として、政治家として、外交政策を研究するのが得意

But my mission this time is just to prevent the Third World War between the Soviet Union and the United States. I made good relations between China and the United States and, after that, made American powers cooperate and surpass the Soviet Union. I settled the Third World War. It was a Cold War. The Cold War never became a hot war. I settled that in 1990 or 1991.

This time, a Korean hot war could have been possible, but I took the next step. It's how to use Chinese power to prevent a North Korean nuclear war. I advised like that. I said, "Mr. Donald Trump, use Chinese power to stop North Korea. It's very essential." I said so, and he obeyed my opinion and succeeded in preventing the nuclear war from occurring. This is the second point.

The third is, of course, a nuclear war between India and Pakistan, and of course, between Iran, Israel, Saudi Arabia, Syria, Turkey, Egypt, and the Middle East. But

です。ただ、私の今世の使命は、ソ連とアメリカの第3次世界大戦をまさに防ぐことでした。私は、中国とアメリカの間によき関係を築き、その後、アメリカの力を団結させ、ソ連を超えるようにしました。こうして、私は第3次世界大戦を解決しました。それは「冷戦」でした。冷戦は、武力を行使する熱い戦争には決してならなかったのです。私は、それを1990年か1991年に解決しました。

今回、朝鮮で熱い戦争が起きる可能性があったのですが、私は、次の手を打ちました。それは、「北朝鮮の核戦争を防ぐために、中国の力をいかに使うか」ということです。そのように私はアドバイスしました。私は、「ドナルド・トランプさん、北朝鮮を押しとどめるためには、中国の力を使うことです。それが非常に重要です」と言いました。私は、そう言いました。そして、彼は私の意見に従い、核戦争の勃発を防ぐことに成功したのです。これが、2番目のポイントです。

3番目は、もちろん、「インドとパキスタンの核戦争」であり、もちろん、「イランやイスラエル、サウジアラビア、シリア、トルコ、エジプトなどの中東の核戦争」です。

it's beyond my power. It's the next age, so I ask you to help me about that. I cannot survive until that time, so please help me about that.

Ayaori Were you born as a prophet in the ancient times?

Kissinger's G.S. Of course. I'm always a prophet. I am in some meaning a coordinator, in another meaning a strategist, sometimes a politician, and sometimes a religious leader.

Ayaori Could you share some names?

Kissinger's G.S. Ah, you should not know the names. I am one of the angels. An angel.

Ayaori Of Christianity?

しかし、これは私の力を超えています。次の時代のことですから、それについては、あなたがたに助けを要請(ようせい)します。そのときまで生きながらえていないでしょうから、それについては私を助けてください。

綾織　あなたは、古代に預言者としてお生まれになったのでしょうか。

キッシンジャー守護霊　もちろんです。私は常に預言者であり、ある意味では調整者であり、ある意味では戦略家であり、時には政治家であり、時には宗教指導者です。

綾織　名前を教えていただけないでしょうか。

キッシンジャー守護霊　ああ、あなたがたは名前を知らないはずですよ。私は天使の一人です。天使です。

綾織　キリスト教の、でしょうか。

Kissinger's G.S. Jewish.

Ayaori Jewish?

Kissinger's G.S. An angel of Jewish origin. One of the cherubim*. Cherubim are the swords of God. There are 12 cherubim. I'm one of them.

Ayaori Thank you very much.

Ichikawa The guardian spirit of Dr. Henry Kissinger, thank you very much for today's session. I'm sure that

キッシンジャー守護霊　ユダヤ教ですね。

綾織　ユダヤ教ですか。

キッシンジャー守護霊　ユダヤ教に由来する天使です。「ケルビム」の一人です。ケルビムは「神の剣」です。ケルビムには12人いますが、私はそのうちの一人です。

綾織　ありがとうございます。

市川　ヘンリー・キッシンジャー博士の守護霊様、本日はまことにありがとうございました。あなたのアドバイスの

● 『旧約聖書』に登場する天使。「創世記」によると、神は、アダムとイブの追放後、エデンの園の東にケルビムと炎の剣を置き、命の木を守らせたという。知識を司るとされ、「智天使」とも訳される。写真（左）は、16世紀に描かれた絵。

* An angel that is mentioned in the *Old Testament*. According to the Genesis, after God drove away Adam and Eve, He placed cherubim and a flaming sword at the east of the garden of Eden to guard the tree of life. He is said to embody wisdom, and is sometimes called cherub. The picture (left) was drawn in the 16th century.

the people of the world must be convinced by your advice. This is the way we should follow. Thank you very much for your advice.

Kissinger's G.S. Thank you very much. I hope, a lot, that you are the right person, the right people, the right party, and the right science for the future. Please help the people of the world. I want to say to Ms. Shaku, "Don't be disappointed. Be brave. Be constructive." Hahahaha. You are young enough, so you must cooperate with each other and do good deeds from now on. Thank you very much.

Ichikawa Thank you very much.

おかげで、世界中の人々が確信を持つことができたはずです。これが私たちの進むべき道です。アドバイスを頂きましたことに感謝申し上げます。

キッシンジャー守護霊　ありがとう。あなたがたは、未来に向けて、正しき人、正しき人々、正しき政党、正しき科学であっていただきたいと強く願っています。どうか世界の人々を助けてあげてください。釈さんには、「がっかりするな。勇気を持ちなさい。建設的でありなさい」と言いたいですね。ハハハハ。あなたがたはまだまだ若いのですから、力を合わせて、今後もいい活動をしていってください。ありがとう。

市川　ありがとうございました。

11 After the Spiritual Interview

Ryuho Okawa (*Claps twice.*) OK. This was the guardian spirit of Henry Kissinger. His opinion was almost the same (as that of Churchill and the guardian spirit of Kim Yo-jong).

He has another strategy regarding world politics. He might be one of my weapons. I think so. His main point was to prevent a nuclear war and now, he talked about the next strategy, I think. After that, we will succeed his work. Thank you very much.

Interviewers Thank you very much.

11　霊言を終えて

大川隆法　（2回手を叩く）はい。ヘンリー・キッシンジャーの守護霊でした。（チャーチルと金与正守護霊と）だいたい同じ意見でしたね。

　彼は、国際政治に関する新たな戦略を持っています。彼は、私の"武器"の一つかもしれません。そのような気がします。中心論点は「核戦争の防止」でしたが、「その先のもの」もあったと思います。そこから先は、私たちが彼の仕事を受け継いでいきましょう。ありがとうございました。

質問者一同　ありがとうございました。

『米朝会談後に世界はどう動くか
キッシンジャー博士 守護霊インタビュー』
大川隆法著作関連書籍

『北朝鮮の実質ナンバー2 金与正の実像
守護霊インタビュー』(幸福の科学出版刊)
『米朝会談後の外交戦略　チャーチルの霊言』(同上)
『ヘンリー・キッシンジャー博士　7つの近未来予言』(同上)
『世界の潮流はこうなる』(幸福実現党刊)
『信仰の法』(幸福の科学出版刊)

米朝会談後に世界はどう動くか
キッシンジャー博士 守護霊インタビュー

2018年6月25日　初版第1刷

著　者　　大　川　隆　法
発行所　　幸福の科学出版株式会社

〒107-0052　東京都港区赤坂2丁目10番14号
TEL(03)5573-7700
https://www.irhpress.co.jp/

印刷・製本　　株式会社 研文社

落丁・乱丁本はおとりかえいたします
©Ryuho Okawa 2018. Printed in Japan. 検印省略
ISBN 9978-4-8233-0012-7 C0030
カバー写真：KCNA/UPI/アフロ／ AFP/アフロ／新華社／アフロ
装丁・写真（上記・パブリックドメインを除く）©幸福の科学

大川隆法霊言シリーズ・最新刊 世界情勢を読む

北朝鮮の実質ナンバー2
金与正の実像
守護霊インタビュー

米朝会談は成功か、失敗か？　北朝鮮の実質ナンバー2である金与正氏守護霊が、世界中のメディアが読み切れない、その衝撃の舞台裏を率直に語った。

1,400円

米朝会談後の外交戦略
チャーチルの霊言

かつてヒットラーから世界を救った名宰相チャーチルによる「米朝会談」客観分析。中国、韓国、ロシアの次の一手を読み、日本がとるべき外交戦略を指南する。

1,400円

守護霊インタビュー
習近平 世界支配へのシナリオ
米朝会談に隠された中国の狙い

米朝首脳会談に隠された中国の狙いとは？　米中貿易戦争のゆくえとは？　覇権主義を加速する中国国家主席・習近平氏の驚くべき本心に迫る。

1,400円

幸福の科学出版

大川隆法 霊言シリーズ・世界の指導者の本心

守護霊インタビュー
トランプ大統領の決意
北朝鮮問題の結末とその先のシナリオ

英語霊言 日本語訳付き

「自分の国は自分で守る」──。日本がその意志を示し、国防体制を築かなければアメリカは守り切れない。世界が注目する"アメリカ大統領の本心"が明らかに。

1,400円

文在寅守護霊 vs. 金正恩守護霊
南北対話の本心を読む

南北首脳会談で北朝鮮は非核化されるのか？ 南北統一、対日米戦略など、対話路線で世界を欺く両首脳の本心とは。外交戦略を見直すための警鐘の一冊。

1,400円

ロシアの本音
プーチン大統領守護霊
vs. 大川裕太

北方領土の返還はなぜ進まないのか。プーチン氏の守護霊が日本を信用できない「本当の理由」を語った。日本外交の未来を占う上で、重要な証言。

1,400円

※表示価格は本体価格(税別)です。

幸福の科学グループのご案内

宗教、教育、政治、出版などの活動を通じて、地球的ユートピアの実現を目指しています。

幸福の科学

1986年に立宗。信仰の対象は、地球系霊団の最高大霊、主エル・カンターレ。世界100カ国以上の国々に信者を持ち、全人類救済という尊い使命のもと、信者は、「愛」と「悟り」と「ユートピア建設」の教えの実践、伝道に励んでいます。

(2018年6月現在)

愛 幸福の科学の「愛」とは、与える愛です。これは、仏教の慈悲や布施の精神と同じことです。信者は、仏法真理をお伝えすることを通して、多くの方に幸福な人生を送っていただくための活動に励んでいます。

悟り 「悟り」とは、自らが仏の子であることを知るということです。教学や精神統一によって心を磨き、智慧を得て悩みを解決すると共に、天使・菩薩の境地を目指し、より多くの人を救える力を身につけていきます。

ユートピア建設 私たち人間は、地上に理想世界を建設するという尊い使命を持って生まれてきています。社会の悪を押しとどめ、善を推し進めるために、信者はさまざまな活動に積極的に参加しています。

海外支援・災害支援

国内外の世界で貧困や災害、心の病で苦しんでいる人々に対しては、現地メンバーや支援団体と連携して、物心両面にわたり、あらゆる手段で手を差し伸べています。

自殺を減らそうキャンペーン

年間約３万人の自殺者を減らすため、全国各地で街頭キャンペーンを展開しています。

公式サイト www.withyou-hs.net

ヘレンの会

ヘレン・ケラーを理想として活動する、ハンディキャップを持つ方とボランティアの会です。視聴覚障害者、肢体不自由な方々に仏法真理を学んでいただくための、さまざまなサポートをしています。

公式サイト www.helen-hs.net

入会のご案内

幸福の科学では、大川隆法総裁が説く仏法真理（ぶっぽうしんり）をもとに、「どうすれば幸福になれるのか、また、他の人を幸福にできるのか」を学び、実践しています。

仏法真理を学んでみたい方へ

大川隆法総裁の教えを信じ、学ぼうとする方なら、どなたでも入会できます。入会された方には、『入会版「正心法語（しょうしんほうご）」』が授与されます。

ネット入会 入会ご希望の方はネットからも入会できます。
happy-science.jp/joinus

信仰をさらに深めたい方へ

仏弟子としてさらに信仰を深めたい方は、仏・法・僧の三宝（ぶっぽうそう さんぽう）への帰依を誓う「三帰誓願式（きがんもん）」を受けることができます。三帰誓願者には、『仏説・正心法語』『祈願文①』『祈願文②』『エル・カンターレへの祈り』が授与されます。

幸福の科学 サービスセンター
TEL 03-5793-1727
受付時間／
火～金：10～20時
土・日祝：10～18時

幸福の科学 公式サイト
happy-science.jp

幸福の科学グループの教育・人材養成事業

教育 ハッピー・サイエンス・ユニバーシティ
Happy Science University

ハッピー・サイエンス・ユニバーシティとは

ハッピー・サイエンス・ユニバーシティ(HSU)は、大川隆法総裁が設立された「現代の松下村塾」であり、「日本発の本格私学」です。
建学の精神として「幸福の探究と新文明の創造」を掲げ、チャレンジ精神にあふれ、新時代を切り拓く人材の輩出を目指します。

学部のご案内

人間幸福学部
人間学を学び、新時代を切り拓くリーダーとなる

経営成功学部
企業や国家の繁栄を実現する、起業家精神あふれる人材となる

未来産業学部
新文明の源流を創造するチャレンジャーとなる

未来創造学部
時代を変え、未来を創る主役となる

政治家やジャーナリスト、ライター、俳優・タレントなどのスター、映画監督・脚本家などのクリエーター人材を育てます。4年制と短期特進課程があります。

・4年制
1年次は長生キャンパスで授業を行い、2年次以降は東京キャンパスで授業を行います。

・短期特進課程(2年制)
1年次・2年次ともに東京キャンパスで授業を行います。

HSU未来創造・東京キャンパス
〒136-0076
東京都江東区南砂2-6-5
TEL **03-3699-7707**

公式サイト
happy-science.university

HSU長生キャンパス
〒299-4325
千葉県長生郡長生村一松丙 4427-1
TEL **0475-32-7770**

幸福の科学グループの教育・人材養成事業

学校法人 幸福の科学学園

学校法人 幸福の科学学園は、幸福の科学の教育理念のもとにつくられた教育機関です。人間にとって最も大切な宗教教育の導入を通じて精神性を高めながら、ユートピア建設に貢献する人材輩出を目指しています。

幸福の科学学園
中学校・高等学校（那須本校）
2010年4月開校・栃木県那須郡（男女共学・全寮制）
TEL 0287-75-7777
公式サイト happy-science.ac.jp

関西中学校・高等学校（関西校）
2013年4月開校・滋賀県大津市（男女共学・寮及び通学）
TEL 077-573-7774
公式サイト kansai.happy-science.ac.jp

仏法真理塾「サクセスNo.1」 TEL 03-5750-0747（東京本校）
小・中・高校生が、信仰教育を基礎にしながら、「勉強も『心の修行』」と考えて学んでいます。

不登校児支援スクール「ネバー・マインド」 TEL 03-5750-1741
心の面からのアプローチを重視して、不登校の子供たちを支援しています。
また、障害児支援の「ユー・アー・エンゼル！」運動も行っています。

エンゼルプランV TEL 03-5750-0757
幼少時からの心の教育を大切にして、信仰をベースにした幼児教育を行っています。

シニア・プラン21 TEL 03-6384-0778
希望に満ちた生涯現役人生のために、年齢を問わず、多くの方が学んでいます。

NPO活動支援

学校からのいじめ追放を目指し、さまざまな社会提言をしています。また、各地でのシンポジウムや学校への啓発ポスター掲示等に取り組む一般財団法人「いじめから子供を守ろうネットワーク」を支援しています。

ブログ blog.mamoro.org
公式サイト mamoro.org
相談窓口 TEL.03-5719-2170

幸福の科学グループ事業

幸福実現党 釈量子サイト
shaku-ryoko.net

[Twitter]
釈量子@shakuryoko
で検索

党の機関紙
「幸福実現NEWS」

政治

幸福実現党

内憂外患（ないゆうがいかん）の国難に立ち向かうべく、2009年5月に幸福実現党を立党しました。創立者である大川隆法党総裁の精神的指導のもと、宗教だけでは解決できない問題に取り組み、幸福を具体化するための力になっています。

幸福実現党 党員募集中

あなたも幸福を実現する政治に参画しませんか。

○ 幸福実現党の理念と綱領、政策に賛同する18歳以上の方なら、どなたでも参加いただけます。
○ 党費：正党員（年額5千円［学生 年額2千円］）、特別党員（年額10万円以上）、家族党員（年額2千円）
○ 党員資格は党費を入金された日から1年間です。
○ 正党員、特別党員の皆様には機関紙「幸福実現NEWS（党員版）」が送付されます。

＊申込書は、下記、幸福実現党公式サイトでダウンロードできます。
住所：〒107-0052　東京都港区赤坂2-10-8 6階 幸福実現党本部
[TEL] 03-6441-0754　[FAX] 03-6441-0764
[公式サイト] hr-party.jp　[若者向け政治サイト] truthyouth.jp

幸福の科学グループ事業

幸福の科学出版

出版メディア事業

大川隆法総裁の仏法真理の書を中心に、ビジネス、自己啓発、小説など、さまざまなジャンルの書籍・雑誌を出版しています。他にも、映画事業、文学・学術発展のための振興事業、テレビ・ラジオ番組の提供など、幸福の科学文化を広げる事業を行っています。

アー・ユー・ハッピー？
are-you-happy.com

ザ・リバティ
the-liberty.com

幸福の科学出版
TEL 03-5573-7700
公式サイト irhpress.co.jp

ザ・ファクト
マスコミが報道しない「事実」を世界に伝えるネット・オピニオン番組

Youtubeにて随時好評配信中！

ザ・ファクト 検索

ニュースター・プロダクション

芸能文化事業

「新時代の"美しさ"」を創造する芸能プロダクションです。2016年3月に映画「天使に"アイム・ファイン"」を、2017年5月には映画「君のまなざし」を公開しています。

公式サイト newstarpro.co.jp

ARI Production
（アリプロダクション）

タレント一人ひとりの個性や魅力を引き出し、「新時代を創造するエンターテインメント」をコンセプトに、世の中に精神的価値のある作品を提供していく芸能プロダクションです。

公式サイト aripro.co.jp

大川隆法　講演会のご案内

　大川隆法総裁の講演会が全国各地で開催されています。
　講演のなかでは、毎回、「世界教師」としての立場から、幸福な人生を生きるための心の教えをはじめ、世界各地で起きている宗教対立、紛争、国際政治や経済といった時事問題に対する指針など、日本と世界がさらなる繁栄の未来を実現するための道筋が示されています。

2017年8月2日 東京ドーム「人類の選択」

2017年5月14日 ロームシアター京都
「永遠なるものを求めて」

2017年4月23日 高知県立県民体育館
「人生を深く生きる」

2018年2月3日 都城市総合文化ホール(宮崎県)
「情熱の高め方」

2017年12月7日 幕張メッセ(千葉県)「愛を広げる力」

講演会には、どなたでもご参加いただけます。
最新の講演会の開催情報はこちらへ。　→

大川隆法総裁公式サイト
https://ryuho-okawa.org